THE FREUD ANNIVERSARY
LECTURE SERIES
THE NEW YORK PSYCHOANALYTIC
INSTITUTE

THE FREUD ANNIVERSARY LECTURE SERIES
The New York Psychoanalytic Institute

DIFFICULTIES
IN THE PATH OF
PSYCHOANALYSIS

A Confrontation of Past with Present Viewpoints

Anna Freud

INTERNATIONAL UNIVERSITIES PRESS, INC.

New York

Delivered as the 18th Freud Anniversary Lecture,
in New York, on April 16, 1968.

Contents

Introduction

Learning from Negative Experience

PSYCHOANALYSIS came into being as a medical psychology, in answer to the lack of adequate therapeutic measures for the treatment of neurotic illnesses. It is this unquestioned historical circumstance which obscures another, much more significant connection between psychopathology and the basic findings of the new discipline. What is referred to here is the fact that none of the latter could have been established while dealing with normal, healthy individuals, in whom the deeper layers of the mind remain securely hidden behind a smooth and often impenetrable surface. Only where functioning is disturbed, does this surface break open sufficiently to allow for glimpses into the depth.

In the *New Introductory Lectures on Psycho-Analysis* (1933), Freud stressed that "we are familiar with the notion that pathology, by making things larger and coarser, can draw our attention to normal conditions which would otherwise have escaped us." He compared *psychotic* patients to crystals which, when broken up, reveal their structure by the manner in which they come apart. These patients, having "turned away from external reality, . . . know more about internal, psychical reality and can reveal a number of things to us that would otherwise be inaccessible to us" (p. 58f.).

Our observations of *neurotic* patients are no less productive of information. The more seriously an individual is torn by conflicts and contradictory forces within himself, the more opportunity he provides for profitable exploration. So long as the defenses set up by a person's ego are intact, the analytic observer is faced by a blank; as soon as they break down, for example, when repression fails and unconscious material returns from the repressed, a mass of information about inner processes becomes available. Likewise, so long as secondary process thinking is maintained undisturbed, the observer's knowledge is restricted to the limited area of the patient's conscious ego; only a return to primary process functioning, as it occurs in dreams, in symptom formation, etc., opens up what in psychoanalysis has been called the "royal road to the unconscious." It is also well known that the regressions which occur in all mental disorders were, and are, the most reliable source of information regarding forward development. So long as an adult individual maintains his sex life on the genital level, the preliminary stages which have led up to it remain obscure; the pregenital organizations, consisting of his oral and anal trends, become visible only in the breakdown products of his sex life, i.e., in his perverse tendencies, his warded-off or indulged-in infantile fantasies, etc. Similarly, the regressions in ego functioning which accompany or follow the libidinal regressions provide many useful pointers to the sequences of ego growth and the gradual building up of the most vital ego functions.

On the basis of such impressions analysts developed a belief in the profitable nature of negative experience and extended this from their dealings with individual patients to their dealings with the public in general. In both instances it seemed that more could be learned from the difficulties, obstacles, and set-backs than from the triumphs, successes, and advances, to whatever degree they were achieved.

Freud himself set the trend by dealing at three

[9]

different junctures with the significance of such adverse and seemingly frustrating experiences. The papers in question are "A Difficulty in the Path of Psycho-Analysis (1917), from which the present lecture borrows its title; "The Resistances to Psycho-Analysis" (1925); and, finally, "Analysis Terminable and Interminable" (1937). While the two first-named papers enumerate and detail the obstacles met by psychoanalysis and its representatives in the world outside, the last one deals with the forces which militate against success in analytic treatments and, to some extent also, with some of the difficulties which arise within the analysts themselves.

Part I

The Public

FREUD'S EARLY papers are not reread often enough by the present generation of analysts to impress them vividly with all the advantages which they enjoy in contrast to their predecessors. A qualified analyst today, especially in the United States, will take it more or less for granted that respect is paid to his intensive training; that this will be an asset when he competes for professional appointments; that he will have no difficulty in building up a practice and earning his living; and that, if he sets out to write, he will encounter no difficulty in finding publishers or editors ready to accept his scientific contributions.

Justified expectations of this kind have to be contrasted with the disbelief, the ridicule, the suspicions, and the professional ostracism to which the first generation of analysts were exposed. They were, in fact, pioneers, not only because they ventured out into the unknown, where they had to break new ground, but also in the sense that their endeavors ran counter to and ignored the conventional restrictions of their time, that they risked their social and professional status, and, last but not least, in many instances gave up a secure and profitable career for financial uncertainties and hardships.

According to Freud's papers, these difficulties in the path of and resistance to psychoanalysis were due to its main findings and principal tenets. Those named by him were the discovery of a *dynamic unconscious,* which destroyed the myth of a "free will" and reduced the position of man to "not being master of his own mind"; the importance attributed to the *instinctual forces,* i.e., sex and aggression in the adult and their preliminary stages in infantile life; the attention paid to psychic phenomena such as *dreams and parapraxes,* which until then had not been considered as deserving serious scientific exploration.

It is interesting and salutary to consider the evanescent nature of objections of this kind and to realize that prejudices which loom large enough in one period to create hardship and to obstruct progress can be pushed aside only half a century later as outdated and insignificant. All the evidence shows that this has happened here.

So far as the theory of the *unconscious* is concerned, of course, it may be maintained that this is still considered alien and unacceptable in some quarters. The Law (with some notable exceptions) still clings to the notion of a "reasonable man," whose actions are wholly controlled by conscious knowledge, a fiction around which the debates concerning responsibility are centered. Academic psychology (again with exceptions) adheres to methods of rigorous evaluating, investigating, surveying, and quantifying, which are aimed at the conscious part of the mind, not at the contributions to it from the unconscious. But, on the whole, such isolated refusals of acceptance highlight rather than detract from what has happened elsewhere. It cannot be denied that for the general public the idea of unconscious motivation of behavior has become almost a commonplace; that contemporary writers have embraced it wholeheartedly; that it has exerted a powerful influence on educational methods and attitudes and changed them almost beyond recognition; that it has altered society's attitude toward mental illness, narrowed the gap between normality and pathology, and showed neurotic, psychosomatic, and delinquent disorders to be part of the common hazards of everybody's life.

This reversal of attitudes is still more conspicuous where the theory of *sex* is concerned. Contrasted with the outspokenness of the Kinsey report (1948), or, for example, the work of William Masters and Virginia Johnson on *Human Sexual Response* (1966), Freud's *Three Contributions to the Theory of Sexuality* (1905) as well as his and other analysts' early papers on the role of sexuality, on sexual aberrations, etc., seem, if anything, discreet and diffident. No comparable storm of indignation has been aroused by the contemporary investigations; and even active experimentation is at present condoned freely as a scientific requirement, whereas mere verbal discussion was condemned in the past as an intolerable affront to the conventions.

Similarly, the myth of the *"innocence of childhood"* has disappeared from the scene without leaving much trace. Parents, educators, and the general public have become willing to have their eyes opened to the available evidence and to accept children for what they are: immature psychic structures, dominated by their emotions, by the search for pleasurable experience, and by the strength of their sexual and aggressive drives.

So far as the theory of *aggression* is concerned, two World Wars and the events of the Hitler regime have underlined and confirmed the psychoanalytic assertion that the aggressive and destructive forces are part of human nature and belong to the basic equipment of the human mind.

Even *dreams* have changed their status from being abstruse and therefore negligible occurrences to that of legitimate phenomena and worthy objects of scientific study and experiment, as the contemporary investigations on "dream deprivation" show.[1]

Taken altogether, no one who believes in an unconscious mind, who explores sex and aggression in adults and children, or who investigates dreams will nowadays be classed as an individual given to mystic leanings, or as an eccentric, or as unduly revolutionary, or even as outstandingly progressive.

Whether and how much the analysts have gained by these changes remains an open ques-

[1] See in this respect the publications by Dement (1960), Kales et al. (1964), Ernest Hartmann (1967), and from the analytic side Charles Fisher (1965).

tion. It is only too well known that new and unexpected difficulties often arise as fast as the familiar ones disappear. In fact, psychoanalysis finds itself today in a changing scene in which new challenges are encountered; these come mainly from three sides.

The most serious of these challenges arises in the area of therapy. At the time when Josef Breuer embarked on the "talking cure" with Anna O., there were no competitors; nor were there any when in due course talking under hypnosis was exchanged for free association. As often as analytic treatments were under fire for being too slow, too laborious, too time-consuming and expensive, patients and their families could aways be sure that there was no alternative, at least not if the then current cold-water treatments, rest cures, and faradizations had already been tried and failed. This, as we know, has changed drastically and by now the therapies available for mental disorders are almost as numerous as those for physical ailments. Organic treatments such as fever therapy, electric shock, brain surgery for the most severe psychoses, the chemical therapies for depression, elation, and the anxieties exist in the field side by side with the many forms of dynamic psychotherapy which are the direct offsprings of analytic thinking. If the latter offer short-cuts to health, family psychiatry and community psychiatry aim at making available to society as a whole facilities for regaining or maintaining mental health, which, in classical analysis, remain reserved for the individual.

Under these changed conditions it is not easy for analytic therapy proper to maintain its status and prestige. Analysts have to admit that where quantitatively massive upheavals of the personality are concerned, such as in the psychoses, the purely psychological methods by themselves are inadequate and the organic and chemical means have the advantage over them. They do not concede the same for the neuroses. In competition with the psychotherapies they are justified to maintain that what they have to offer is unique, i.e., thoroughgoing personality changes as compared with more superficial symptomatic cures. Unfortunately, the former is not always aspired to by the patients who aim above all at immediate relief from suffering.

In this struggle to maintain their own standards, analysts are apt to forget that they also hold another card which is not matched by any of the other treatments. Especially the psychotherapies can apply to the individual patient only what is already known about his particular disturbance, limited as such knowledge is still in our times. It is only the psychoanalytic method itself which offers patient and therapist the opportunity to explore further, to add to the existing information, and thereby to increase the individual's chances to find the way to his own cure.

The second new challenge which analysts have to meet is closely connected with the altered status of analysis in the scientific world. So long as psychoanalysis was shunned and looked down on by other disciplines, it was not difficult for its representatives to remain wholly identified with their own field and proudly conscious of their own achievements. There was no occasion to feel, or act, otherwise. This changed when acceptance, or part acceptance, by the outside world opened up the possibility for cooperation, with psychiatry, medicine, education, academic psychology, the social sciences, the law, etc. The advance was welcome, of course, insofar as it realized the hopes and ambitions of the founder of psychoanalysis to have psychoanalysis grow beyond the therapeutic area and see its findings applied to the whole field of human concerns. But it also became a hazard since it lured many analysts away from their own base and created the temptation of being no longer an outsider, of becoming "recognized."

The danger inherent in this attitude is obvious, especially when analysts aspire to the distinction of being on a par with academic psychologists and to realize this ambition not merely by extending their explorations from abnormal to normal functioning but by adopting the academic methods of research, which prove unsuitable for their specific material. It is not unusual to find that analysts nowadays feel more eager to achieve standing and prestige in an allied field than in their own; or that they begin to deplore, secretly or openly, the essentially "unscientific" nature of their discipline which does not allow for laboratory work, for confirmation of findings by experiment and control groups, and, above all, which employs the mind of the explorer as its only scientific instrument, a tool which in the eyes of the critics sadly lacks in objectivity.

For many analysts in this situation, it is not easy to keep the right balance between an overstrict isolationism, which leaves psychoanalysis stranded, and an overeager collaboration, which threatens the analyst's own professional and scientific image and ideals.

[19]

The third new challenge to psychoanalysis is of a completely different nature. It concerns the changes in the appeal that analysis has for the various sections of the population and its consequences for recruitment.

When we scrutinize the personalities who, by self-selection, became the first generation of psychoanalysts, we are left in no doubt about their characteristics. They were the unconventional ones, the doubters, those who were dissatisfied with the limitations imposed on knowledge; also among them were the odd ones, the dreamers, and those who knew neurotic suffering from their own experience. This type of intake has altered decisively since psychoanalytic training has become institutionalized and appeals in this stricter form to a different type of personality. Moreover, self-selection has given way to the careful scrutiny of applicants, resulting in the exclusion of the mentally endangered, the eccentrics, the self-made, those with excessive flights of imagination, and favoring the acceptance of the sober, well-prepared ones, who are hardworking enough to wish to better their professional efficiency.

Apart from recruitment itself, there are other changes in the scene. Many people feel that psychoanalysis is in danger of losing the allegiance of the young, which was very pronounced at one time, especially after the First World War and in the early '20s of the century when Siegfried Bernfeld propounded the revelations of psychoanalysis to large audiences drawn from the Youth Movement. The young then avidly received and eagerly, often secretly, discussed them as the embodiment of the spirit of change, the contempt for the conventions, freedom of thought about sex and, in the minds of many, the eagerly looked-for prospect of release from sexual restrictions.

This has changed, because the young of today feel that psychoanalysis is now in the hands of the parent generation and as such suspect. For many of them it has lost the aspect of being dangerous, a forbidden matter, accessible only to the courageous, a useful weapon with which to attack society; instead psychoanalysis is looked on and avoided as a procedure devised to deprive them of originality and revolutionary spirit and induce them to adapt and conform to existing conditions, which is the last aim they have in mind.

There is still another and more important dimension to this wholesale or partial disillusionment of the young with psychoanalysis. After all, analysis never offered anything except en-

[21]

lightenment about the inner world, about man's struggle within himself, about his being his own worst enemy. This conflicts with the present battle cry of youth of "man against society." But, perhaps, it has always been true that it is easier and more congenial for the adolescents to lash out against external restrictions than to struggle for internal balance. This latter fight for freedom may be acceptable to them only when it simultaneously serves the purpose of offending the real or alleged susceptibilities of the older generation.

To scrutinize and learn from the obstacles which divide psychoanalysis from the world at large does not imply the opinion that analysts should spend time and effort to improve these relations. On the contrary, experience has shown that such attempts are, at best, ineffective and, at worst, disastrous. No amount of enthusiasm, or of eloquence, or of proselytizing spirit will convince those who hold different opinions. Any analyst who goes too far out of his way to change the world in this respect may end up with meeting the demands of the world by changing the analytic theory or therapeutic procedure.

Part II

The Patients

DIFFICULTIES AS SEEN IN 1937 BY FREUD IN "ANAL-
YSIS TERMINABLE AND INTERMINABLE"

ACCORDING TO James Strachey (1964), Freud "was always well aware of the barriers to success in analysis and was always ready to investigate them" (p. 212). Not that this readiness was an asset so far as the reputation of analysis was concerned. Whenever the possibility of failure in analytic treatment was referred to by anybody, all analysts were accused of therapeutic nihilism, or at least of lack of therapeutic interest and ambition. Whenever Freud, or others, delineated carefully the scope of analytic efficiency, they laid themselves open to the reproach that they themselves did not believe in their own efforts. Nevertheless, the tradition to pay attention to and to learn from negative experience maintained itself intact and the obstacles to analytic therapy which are encountered in the individual patient remained the legitimate focus of the analyst's attention.

When Freud wrote, "Instead of an enquiry how a cure by analysis comes about, . . . the question should be asked of what are the obstacles that stand in the way of such a cure" (p. 221), he did not do so with the patients' common "resistances" in mind. These resistances stem on the one hand from the ego's attempt to maintain the *status quo* of defense, on the other hand from the id's stubborn clinging to distorted forms of satisfaction. Such counterforces are inevitable in every analytic treatment, are dealt with and dissolved within the analytic process, and, far from being obstacles, prove to be, when interpreted, next to the transference the best and most fruitful material on the way to analytic cures.

It was not these but other more subtle and less obvious interferences Freud had in mind when he embarked on their exploration in "Analysis Terminable and Interminable."

Looking for the factors "which are prejudicial to the effectiveness of analysis and make its duration interminable," his first choice were the *quantitative* ones which determine the libido economy within a given individual and are decisive for his inner equilibrium, i.e., for the balance or imbalance in the defensive struggle between id and ego. Any excessive strength of instinct whether constitutionally given or due to developmental reinforcement (puberty, menopause) may make it more difficult or may make it impossible for analysis to achieve its main task, i.e., to "tame" the instincts. Any weakening of the ego, "whether through illness or exhaustion, or from some similar cause" may have the same effect (p. 226).

Next in Freud's enumeration came the *qualitative* factors such as the alterations in the ego —whether "original, innate" or "acquired during the defensive struggle of the earliest years" (p. 240)—which, for example, determine the individual's selection from the possible mechanisms of defense and may restrict his advances from the primitive to the more sophisticated ones. Named here were also other characteristics such as a "special adhesiveness of the libido"; or an "excessive mobility" of it; or, as a characteristic difficult to localize in the mental apparatus, a "depletion of the plasticity," an amount of "psychical inertia," which makes the personality even of young patients "fixed and rigid" and prevents them from benefiting from the possibilities for change that are opened up by analytic therapy (p. 242f.).

To these obstacles to success in analysis, Freud added others "which may spring from different and deeper roots." Foremost among these he named the not infrequent and, by the analyst, dreaded *negative therapeutic reaction* which had frequently been alluded to in earlier publications. He was well aware of the fact that patients during analytic treatment experience not only improvements but also exacerbations of their symptomatology, and this for a variety of reasons. He pointed to the inevitable risk of reducing the defenses of the patient who then has to meet formerly warded-off distressing id material without the relief afforded to him by the use of denial or repression; or to the obstinacy of patients (such as the Wolf Man) who increase the intensity of their symptoms even after interpretation before they can concede to the analyst the victory of having dissolved them; or to those patients who cannot permit themselves to be successful in any endeavor (including the therapeutic one) since for them success as such has acquired the symbolic meaning of fulfillment of a prohibited infantile wish.

Nevertheless, after discussing them, Freud

dismissed these difficulties as less important and, in the majority, amenable to interpretation, and turned to other "negative" reactions which he considered more formidable. These are attributable to guilt, conscious or unconscious, to the need for punishment, and to moral masochism, all of which find their satisfaction in the very fact of neurotic suffering and defy the analyst's efforts to deprive them of this gratification.[1] The severe difficulties encountered in the analysis of such patients, Freud referred to as "the intervention of an element of free aggressiveness," i.e., a quantity of aggressive and destructive energy which the individual has withdrawn from use against the external world and turned inward. In this internalized form, it increases the tendency to internal conflict "irrespective of the quantity of libido" (p. 244). The result is a change in the instinctual climate itself, i.e., an ominous alteration from the search for pleasure as a governing principle to the preference for unpleasure. The latter then dominates mental functioning in the form of masochism.

In addition to this "negative therapeutic reaction," Freud also named as responsible for "interminable" analyses two factors which are

[1] See in this respect Freud (1923, pp. 49-51; 1924; 1930).

rooted in the bisexual nature of human individuals. Men dread and ward off persistently their own feminine leanings toward other males and the resultant "rebellious overcompensation" may prove victorious over all analytic efforts. Above all, it produces an almost impenetrable transference-resistance toward an analyst of the same sex and militates against the acceptance of a cure from him. Similarly, female patients, on the basis of their inherent masculine tendencies, may cling stubbornly to their wish for a penis and, instead of being cured by the treatment, may become severely depressed when they realize that the analysis can do nothing to fulfill this fantasy.

In an informative Editor's Note to Freud's expositions, James Strachey (1964) summarized that "The paper as a whole gives an impression of pessimism in regard to the therapeutic efficacy of psycho-analysis." He attributed this pessimism to the circumstance that the obstacles alluded to "are of a physiological and biological nature" and "thus in the main unsusceptible to psychological influences," as, for example, the "relative 'constitutional' strength of the instincts"; "the relative weakness of the ego owing to physiological causes"; the death instinct as being "actually the ultimate cause of conflict in the mind" (p. 211f.).

On the other hand, he also saw some more hopeful signs in Freud's remarks concerning a therapeutic alteration of the patient's ego. While earlier papers had stressed that, to achieve success in an analytic cure, the ego has to be capable of being strengthened, of being made "more independent of the super-ego," of being "widened" concerning its field of perception, "enlarged" in its organization, able to "appropriate fresh portions of the id" (Freud, 1933, p. 80), it was indicated here for the first time how such alterations could be effected. Due to the recent advances in Freud's analysis of the ego, such therapeutic changes were now seen "as the undoing of alterations already present as results of the defensive process" (p. 213).

Strachey did not stress the fact that, with Freud, a negative note crept into this subject as well. Freud was convinced that not every patient's ego lends itself to improvements of this kind. For these to come about, the ego has to be basically a normal one and "a normal ego . . . is . . . an ideal fiction. . . . Every normal [person's] ego approximates to that of the psychotic in some part or other and to a greater or lesser extent" (p. 235).[2] Thus, on this ground, too, pessimism remained and the impression was left that there are impasses which limit the extent of analytic cures and confront the analyst with problems for which no satisfactory solution was at hand, at least not at the time.

DEVELOPMENTS SINCE 1937

It is well worth our while to inquire what has happened in this particular field in the intervening thirty years; whether additions have been made to Freud's enumeration of difficulties; what remedies have been suggested; and where the latter has happened, whether the solutions found are technically and theoretically tenable and satisfactory.

Additions to the List of Difficulties

What I mention in this respect are personal impressions of my own collected in the field of

[2] Freud's statements in this respect have been fully confirmed since by Charles Brenner (1968), who singles out "Archaic Features in Ego Functioning" and stresses that the very ego capacity on which the analytic technique relies most heavily, i.e., the *synthetic function,* is the one which is most often found wanting; that even so-called normal people may be able to accommodate in their functioning far-reaching inconsistencies and contradictions without feeling the need to confront them with each other, to reach compromises between them or to embark on any other of the possible ways of their integration within the area of the conscious ego.

child analysis. While dealing with children ana-
lytically, it has struck me that certain factors
can be recognized as being significant for the
success or failure of analytic therapy. Other
pathological circumstances being equal, children seem to me less able to respond favorably
if one or more or all of the following four characteristics are present in them:

1. *A low threshold of tolerance for the frustration of instinctual wishes.* Where this is present, any postponement or reduction of gratification becomes particularly intolerable. The
quantities of unpleasure released by frustration
are greater than normal and there is increased
pressure toward immediate discharge of tension; this militates against the gradual modifica-
tion and "taming" of instincts, which is named
by Freud as the major aim of analytic therapy.

2. *A low threshold of tolerance for anxiety.*
This manifests itself adversely in two ways.
First, the less anxiety an individual can tolerate, the quicker he has to resort to defensive
activity and symptom formation, i.e., the worse
are his chances of maintaining or regaining his
mental equilibrium. Secondly, he is badly
equipped for meeting the quantities of anxiety
which are released by the analytic process itself
(through undoing defenses) and for making

constructive use of them. Where anxiety tolerance is too low, interpretation of unconscious
contents induces panic instead of bringing relief.

3. *A low sublimation potential.* Where the
ability to accept substitute gratification is not
intact or where the person has not developed
beyond primitive, crude, material needs, there
are few pathways for displaced discharge and
consequently it becomes more difficult to "tame"
the instincts. Analytic therapy can liberate sub-
limations which are blocked by inhibitions and
defenses; it is another, so far unanswered question whether it can also increase the sublimation potential and thereby improve the patient's
chance to profit from analysis.

4. *Preponderance of regressive over progressive tendencies.* Psychoanalytic therapy applied
to children counts heavily on the intactness of
the wish to "move forward and complete development" (Edward Bibring, 1936). Where this
is deficient, or outweighed by regressive forces,
analysis is used by the child not to resolve developmental arrests but as a licence to return to
earliest levels of id satisfaction and ego expression, i.e., to effect regressions which are not in
the "service of the ego" and may defy the ana-

lyst's effort to use them in the service of the analytic treatment.[3]

Suggested Remedies

The suggestions for improvement of analytic efficiency which have sprung up in the analytic world at large can be divided roughly into two categories, each of which has a link with Freud's own remarks. They take their starting point on the one hand from the "therapeutic alteration of the ego" demanded by him, on the other hand from the notion that the ego distortions which hinder analysis are acquired by the individual during his *earliest* defensive struggle against unpleasure.

As regards the need for a *therapeutic normalization of the ego* during the analytic process, and for the benefit of it, this was immediately taken up and acted on by many of Freud's co-workers and pupils. To quote only a few among many, past and present: that it is one of the aims of analysis to change the relations of the ego to id and superego (Edward Bibring, 1937); that in analysis the ego is induced to stop or

[3] For a more detailed discussion of these four points, see Anna Freud, *Normality and Pathology in Childhood* (1965, Chapter 4).

alter defenses and to tolerate id derivatives which are less and less distorted (Otto Fenichel, 1937); that the analytic technique is devised, point by point, to fit the capabilities of a normal ego and that technical parameters become necessary to match deviations from the norm until these are corrected therapeutically (K. R. Eissler, 1953); that the ego has to be made more tolerant (Strachey, 1934, 1937); that the intrapsychic modifications brought about by analysis have to include the ego (Gill, 1954); that "permanent changes" have to be effected in the ego, "thereby extending [its] power and sovereignty" (Greenson, 1958).

Actually, this increased emphasis on the analysis of the ego (sometimes referred to as "defense analysis") brought with it no major changes of analytic technique. It served merely to stress points which had been made before, but had not always been implemented seriously enough: that, during the analytic process, defense has to be interpreted before the id content which is warded off by it; that to approach id contents without that precaution amounts to "wild" analysis; that the analyst's attention has to be divided equally between content and defense and continually turn from one to the other; that regression in the transference brings with it not only the fantasies and anxieties of infantile life but also the modes of functioning and expression which were characteristic of the past, i.e., that it enlightens analyst and patient not only with regard to past emotional experience but also with regard to past ego functioning, including its deficiencies.

The increased attention paid to the ego during the therapeutic process brought to an end the period when analysis was alluded to exclusively as a depth psychology and turned it into "analysis of the total personality" in the true sense of the term. There is no doubt that this improvement of technique helped the analyst in many cases and was the factor that made it possible to include "character analysis" in the scope of analytic therapy.

The analysis of the ego for therapeutic purposes was linked, further, with Heinz Hartmann's studies of the ego which began in the early '30s of this century. Heinz Hartmann oriented his investigations toward the origin of the ego, the development of its psychological apparatuses, its energy problems, its adaptive function, i.e., toward the sphere outside the id-ego conflicts. Although he did not intend his theoretical findings to have a direct impact on the practice of psychoanalysis, their indirect consequences for the analysts' technical attitudes were considerable.

So far as my personal contributions go, I was wholly identified with the ventures into defense analysis. In fact, in *The Ego and the Mechanisms of Defense* (1936), I was already leaning heavily in this direction.

The second of the suggested remedies is of a different nature.

When Freud wrote of *earliest* defensive struggles or of analyzing the prehistory of the oedipus complex, what he had in mind, probably were events of the anal and oral phases, the period immediately after ego and id had separated off from each other. There is little or no evidence that he thought it possible to deal therapeutically with preverbal experience, in spite of his knowledge and conviction that this is an all-important period in individual life when essential lines for development are laid down, when reaction patterns are preformed, and when basic deprivations and frustrations exert an influence which threatens to be lasting.[4]

Departing from this position, a considerable cross-section of the psychoanalytic community today pins their faith on the analysis of the first

[4] See also M. Balint (1958) on "basic faults."

Sam Yott   1/6/70

Start card.

year of life, with the purpose of therapeutically modifying the impact of the earliest happenings. Freud's discovery that every neurosis of the adult is preceded by an infantile neurosis and that the latter has to be analyzed before the former can be reached, is paraphrased by them as follows: every infantile neurosis in the oedipal period is preceded by fateful interactions between infant and mother in the very first days and months of life, and it is this archaic, preverbal phase which has to be revived in the transference and analyzed before the later infantile neurosis can be approached effectively.

This view is held today by many analysts of otherwise widely divergent opinions.[5] Interestingly enough, it has been described systematically, not by a member of one of the more independent and revolutionary analytic sections, but by Jeanne Lampl-de Groot, a representative of the classical analytic approach. In a recent paper "On Obstacles Standing in the Way of Psychoanalytic Cure" (1967), she goes through the list of difficulties cited by Freud, referring each back to some happening during the earliest mother-infant interaction: the (masochistic) *negative therapeutic reaction* of some patients who have a need for self-punishment, to "the

[5] See, for example, René Spitz, D. W. Winnicott, Melanie Klein, Herbert Rosenfeld and others.

primitive fear of their own aggressive drives and the destruction of their omnipotence fantasies" directed against the mother; the *incapacity to tame the instinctual drives,* to the modes of drive discharge initiated when the ego is helpless vis-à-vis the drives and "strongly dependent on the mother's support"; *irregular and distorted ego development,* to failures in the original dyad between infant and mother; the *bisexual problems,* to the infant's fear of merging with a dominating mother, a fear of passivity which later, in the phallic phase, acquires sexual meaning.

Any attempt to carry analysis from the verbal to the preverbal period of development brings with it practical and technical innovations as well as theoretical implications, many of which are controversial.

What strikes the observer first is a change in the type of *psychic material* with which the analysis is dealing. Instead of exploring the disharmonies between the various agencies within a structured personality, the analyst is concerned with the events which lead from the chaotic, undifferentiated state toward the initial building up of a psychic structure. This means going beyond the area of intrapsychic conflict, which had always been the legitimate target for psychoanalysis, and into the darker area of interaction between innate endowment and environmental influence. The implied aim is to undo or to counteract the impact of the very forces on which the rudiments of personality development are based.

Analysts who work for this aim assure us that this can be achieved. They feel enthusiastic about the new therapeutic prospects which they see opening out before them. Jeanne Lampl-de Groot, in her paper, confesses to being "far from optimistic" in cases in which the damage done during the initial mother-infant interaction has been massive. I myself cannot help feeling doubtful about trying to advance into the area of primary repression, i.e., to deal with processes which, by nature, are totally different from the results of the ego's defensive maneuvers with which we feel familiar.

As regards *technique,* it is obvious that different methods are needed for the approach to the earliest rather than to the later phases. Lampl-de Groot mentions "nonverbal modes of communication" which become unavoidable. Others speak of "silent communion" between analyst and patient, or use other terms to stress the need for the analyst's intuitive understanding of the patient's signs and signals, his empathy, etc. However that may be, there is no doubt that neither memory nor verbal recall reach into the depth of postnatal, preverbal experience. Therefore, remembering yields its place to repetition, verbal communication to re-enactment. This explains the heightened significance of communication via the transference in many present-day analyses, where transference interpretations are considered the only therapeutically effective ones and where the transference phenomena are perforce given preference over memory, free association, and dreams, as the only real road to the unconscious.

It is, in fact, this central and unique role given to the transference in the psychoanalytic process, to the exclusion of all other avenues of communication, which is, to date, one of the points of controversy in the analytic world. There is, further, the question whether the transference really has the power to transport the patient back as far as the beginning of life. Many are convinced that this is the case. Others, myself among them, raise the point that it is one thing for preformed, object-related fantasies to return from repression and be redirected from the inner to the outer world (i.e., to the person of the analyst); but that it is an entirely different, almost magical expectation to have the patient in analysis change back into the prepsychological, undifferentiated, and unstructured state, in which no divisions exist between body and mind or self and object.

The argument that it is the quality of the analytic setting itself which promotes such deep regressions also does not necessarily command belief. In many respects, the mother-infant and the analyst-patient relationship are dissimilar rather than similar. What is characteristic for the former is the infant's need for an ever-present, exclusive, timelessly devoted, giving and comforting partner, while the latter is characterized by the existence of rivals, restriction in time, demands for punctuality and cooperation, release of anxiety, withholding of reassurance, frustration of wishes, at best token gratifications. Taken altogether, the question is left open whether, in fact, the re-enactment of life after birth does, or does not, take place in the patient's mind.

Another controversial point concerns the role of the ego within the analytic process. In the classical procedure, as described above, this role is considered decisive in various respects: for the initial pact with the analyst; for the patient's willingness to reduce or suspend defenses and thereby promote upsurges from the id; for accepting insight; for incorporating the result of interpretations within its own organization, etc. Furthermore, the aim itself of analysis is geared to the concept of a mediating ego that is helped to abandon defensive structures built up in infantile life on faulty premises and to replace them by more adequate and rational solutions.

Perhaps it has never been spelt out explicitly that such considerations cease to apply where analysis aims to penetrate into pre-ego strata, where the power of a quasi-delusional transference is meant to carry the patient far beyond the confines of ego functioning into the reliving of primary emotional experience. What is expected of the ego under these altered circumstances is not only the undoing of its own faulty moves but also the undoing of the impact of the very processes which have led to its formation.

More important than these mainly technical considerations seem to me *two theoretical assumptions* which are implied in them.

The first of these is a revision of the distinction between inherited and acquired characteristics. According to Freud (1937), "We have no reason to dispute the existence and importance of original, innate distinguishing characteristics of the ego" (p. 240), which, is, after all, initially, one with the id. Nevertheless, the extent of an individual's innate endowment has been under dispute in recent years, based partly on psycho-analytic reconstructions, partly on the direct observation of mother-child couples. Both types of data have produced in us the conviction that much that used to be considered innate can now be shown to have been acquired during the first year of life and to have been added to the inherited constitution.[6]

But if there is unanimous agreement on this point, there is, in contrast, vivid disagreement concerning a theoretical inference drawn from it. The new technical proposals aimed at the beginning of life imply the assumption that whatever is acquired is reversible. This is by no means proved. It may well be that the very basis on which personality formation rests is, in fact, bedrock.

[6] On this point see also Martin James (1960) and others.

Part III

The Analysts

THAT THE smoothness of the analytic process is interfered with not only by the patients' resistances and negative reactions but also by flaws in the analysts' abilities and personalities belongs to basic knowledge. It has come under scrutiny at all times under various titles such as a general lack of sensitivity to the unconscious, blind spots due to the analyst's own repressions, countertransference reactions, etc. In "Analysis Terminable and Interminable" Freud mentioned as unfortunate for the outcome of analysis if the analyst does not possess "a considerable degree of mental normality and correctness," "some kind of superiority," a basic "love of truth" (p. 248). He alerted analysts to the danger of having their own instinctual demands stirred up by constant preoccupation with the patients' repressed material and then either strengthening their defenses by diverting "the implications and demands of analysis from themselves" or by permitting themselves in action the freedom which they grant to their patients in free thought and association.

Jeanne Lampl-de Groot (1967), following René Spitz (1965), lays special stress on the need for intactness of the analyst's receptive empathy, a mode of functioning which is frequently blocked early in life, by repression of the resentment caused by the mother's interference with the infant's "need to become a person in his own right" (p. 32). The harmful consequences of unchecked countertransference have been emphasized by many authors, Paula Heimann (1950) foremost among them. That only the analyst's own preparatory analysis can combat these defects is a general opinion, although only Freud (1937) carried this conviction far enough to recommend that "Every analyst should periodically—at intervals of five years or so—submit himself to analysis once more, without feeling ashamed of taking this step" (p. 249).

In addition to these time-honored concerns about the analysts' therapeutic activities, new ones have recently come into the foreground with regard to the analysts' literary output and the impact of the quality of these publications on the future of psychoanalysis. In some quarters, notably in the American Psychoanalytic Association, these have been taken so seriously that an "Ad Hoc Committee for Scientific Activities"[1] has been set up to explore the situation. An official Report (1967) of this Committee emphasizes that "while there exists a good deal of productive investigative activity in the peripheral and applied fields, there is deficiency of creative research in the central areas of psychoanalysis, which, if it is not remedied, might in the long run constitute a threat to the survival of psychoanalysis as a science." Discussing the central areas of psychoanalysis, Heinz Kohut stresses that among the contributions to man's understanding of himself, "what is specific for analysis is that the increase in knowledge and the subsequent potential increase in mastery (1) concern the inner life of man, and (2) are the result of an expansion of the territory of the ego, i.e., specifically due to transformations from infantile forms of automatic pain avoidance to tension tolerance and reality acceptance."[2]

In the face of the dangers which are foreseen, not for the extension but for the intensification

[1] Members: Heinz Kohut, Chairman; A. Russell Anderson, Grete L. Bibring, Douglas D. Bond, John E. Gedo, Seymour L. Lustman, Peter B. Neubauer.

[2] From a letter to Douglas Bond, June 3, 1967. Quoted with the writer's permission.

of the psychoanalytic theory, the Committee members make suggestions how to promote *creative research, scientific progress,* and *productivity* among analysts. They also raise the question whether whatever is lacking in these respects in the present analytic scene is due to the methods of selecting candidates for analytic training (in the United States: restriction to medically trained individuals with the exclusion of potentially creative minds from allied fields); or to the training methods themselves (which have become institutionalized and are, on the whole, restricted to matters of technique and therapy); or to the general atmosphere in the analytic communities (where professional success and advancement are often priced more highly than patient scientific exploration).

Although I personally find it easy to identify wholeheartedly with the aims and objects of this Committee, the answers with which I myself come up are of a different nature. I do not believe that either selection or training methods, or Society trends can severely interfere with creativity. There has been a profusion of creative minds in modern medicine, even if in the organic field; moreover, creative individuals are usually the revolutionary ones whose spirits are not easily subdued by whatever is imposed on them, first by their teachers, later by their professional colleagues. Besides, it may be an error altogether to think of these developments in terms of creativity. The analyst's task is not to create, i.e., to invent anything, but to observe, to explore, to understand, and to explain. It is in respect to these latter activities that an important quality appears to me in danger of getting lost.

Psychoanalytic thinking, in classical terms, implied the specific demand that every clinical fact should be approached from four aspects: *genetically,* as to its origin; *dynamically,* as to the interplay of forces of which it is the result; *economically,* with regard to its energy charge; *topographically* (later *structurally*), concerning its localization within the mental apparatus.[3] It was the psychology based on this view of mental functioning which was singled out by the name of *metapsychology.*

Nevertheless, in our times, the term metapsychology has assumed a very different meaning. What it denotes now is largely theory building, distant from the area of clinical material, an activity which demands and is reserved for a specific, speculative quality of mind. As such it

[3] A fifth aspect, the *adaptive* one to be added later; see Hartmann (1939) and Rapaport and Gill (1959).

has become the bugbear of the clinically oriented analyst who feels wholly divorced from it. This brings about a division which, in the long run, threatens both areas with sterility: the theoretical field due to the absence of clinical data, the clinical field due to a diminution in their theoretical evaluation and exploration. What is lost, finally, is what used to be considered as a *sine qua non* in psychoanalysis: the essential *unity* between clinical and theoretical thinking.

A look at the history of the four metapsychological aspects may take us a step further. Although they were meant to exist and be developed simultaneously, this did not happen according to intention. There were always periods when one or the other of them gained ascendancy to the comparative detriment of the remaining ones.

The first to be given widespread approval was, no doubt, the *dynamic* aspect. In fact, to approach mental functioning and mental illness in terms of conflict between opposing forces seemed so obvious and acceptable, not only to the analysts themselves, that for a while it dominated the scene and became the hallmark of enlightened thinking, especially in psychiatry.

On this basis, psychoanalysis used to be alluded to as a "dynamic psychology." This, of course, disregarded the fact that in metapsychological thinking an interplay of internal forces as such remains inconclusive unless information is added where in the mental apparatus these forces are localized; whether they possess the same or different psychical qualities (unconscious, preconscious, conscious); whether they are able to meet each other on the same level and within the same mental area; to reduce each other; to enter into compromises with each other, etc.; or whether they are walled off from each other by defensive activity. In short, the dynamic point of view is not profitable for the analyst, except in combination with the *topographical* one. But acceptance of the latter was more hesitant and less wholehearted and did not become prominent in the analytic literature until 1926 when *Inhibitions, Symptoms and Anxiety* put it into the foreground in its revised form as the *"structural* aspect."

There was never any doubt about psychoanalysis as a *genetic* psychology. The genetic point of view had a recognized existence from the moment when psychoanalytic exploration turned from the neurotic problems of adult life to their forerunners in childhood and demonstrated the impact of early on later happenings and patterns.

In contrast, the *economic* aspect had a chequered career and not only because "the term 'mental energy' may give rise to criticism on the part of psychologists, psychiatrists, and psychoanalysts" (Lampl-de Groot, 1967, p. 24). Freud himself was always convinced of the highly important part quantity plays in the defensive struggles against unpleasure which go on in the mental apparatus early in life and play havoc with the normality of the ego. He was equally convinced of the fact that the outcome of every analytic treatment depends essentially on quantitative factors, i.e., on the strength of the patient's resistances and negative reactions measured against the amounts of energy upon which analysis can draw. Nevertheless, he admitted with regret that "our theoretical concepts have neglected to attach the same importance to the *economic* line of approach as they have to the *dynamic* and *topographical* ones" (1937, p. 226f.).

To return from here to the analysts of today and the problems of present and future development of analytic thinking:

What may give rise to concern is a comparative neglect of the fact that the relations of the four metapsychological aspects to the notion of a psychoanalytic cure are not on an equal level. While alterations of the economics, dynamics, and structure of the patient's personality are the essence of analytic therapy, exploration of the genetic roots is not the aim in itself but the means to the end of understanding and interpretation. Heinz Hartmann, who in psychoanalysis is the genetic explorer par excellence, expressed this very succinctly when in 1939 he wrote concerning his own efforts to disentangle the roots of ego development: "Many of these lengthy . . . considerations are not psychoanalytic in the narrow sense, and some of them seem to have taken us quite far from the core of psychoanalysis" (p. 108).

However that may be, one look at the analytic scene of today can convince us that the desire to unearth ever earlier and deeper antecedents, not only of the ego but of human emotions, anxieties, and struggles in general, has taken hold of the analysts' imagination. For the moment it outstrips most other interests, and it may take some time until the other metapsychological aspects catch up again with the genetic one which has strayed ahead.

But this, exactly, is what we should be waiting for. The newly discovered facts about early and earliest life need to fall into place within the dynamics, the economy, and the structure of the personalities for which they prepare the ground. Only in this way can metapsychology regain its former status. It is also only in this way that we shall approach once more what the Ad Hoc Committee for Scientific Activities calls hopefully

"a creative era in psychoanalysis."

References

Balint, M. (1958), The Three Areas of the Mind. *International Journal of Psycho-Analysis,* 39:328-340.

Bibring, E. (1936), The Development and Problems of the Theory of the Instincts. *International Journal of Psycho-Analysis,* 22:102-131, 1941.

———(1937), On the Theory of the Therapeutic Results of Psycho-Analysis. *International Journal of Psycho-Analysis,* 18:170-189.

Brenner, C. (1968), Archaic Features of Ego Functioning. *International Journal of Psycho-Analysis,* 49:426-429.

Breuer, F. & Freud, S. (1893-1895), Studies on Hysteria. *Standard Edition,* 2. London: Hogarth Press, 1955.

Dement, W. (1960), Effect of Dream Deprivation. *Science,* 131:1705-1707.

———& Fisher, C. (1963), Experimental Interference with the Sleep Cycle. *Canadian Psychiatric Association Journal,* 8:400-405.

Eissler, K. R. (1953), The Effect of the Structure of

the Ego on Psychoanalytic Technique. *Journal of the American Psychoanalytic Association,* 1:104-143.

Fenichel, O. (1937), Symposium on the Theory of the Therapeutic Results of Psychoanalysis. *The Collected Papers of Otto Fenichel,* 2:19-24. New York: Norton, 1954.

Fisher, C. (1965), Psychoanalytic Implications of Recent Research on Sleep and Dreaming. *Journal of the American Psychoanalytic Association,* 13: 197-303.

———& Dement, W. (1963), Studies on Psychopathology of Sleep and Dreams. *American Journal of Psychiatry,* 119:1160-1168.

Freud, Anna (1936), *The Ego and the Mechanisms of Defense* [The Writings of Anna Freud, Vol. II]. New York: International Universities Press, 1966.

———(1965), *Normality and Pathology in Childhood* [The Writings of Anna Freud, Vol. VI]. New York: International Universities Press.

Freud, Sigmund (1905), Three Essays on the Theory of Sexuality. *Standard Edition,* 7:125-243. London: Hogarth Press, 1953.

———(1911-1915), Papers on Technique. *Standard Edition,* 12:85-173. London: Hogarth Press, 1958.

———(1917), A Difficulty in the Path of Psycho-Analysis. *Standard Edition,* 17:135-144. London: Hogarth Press, 1955.

———(1923), The Ego and the Id. *Standard Edition,* 19:3-66. London: Hogarth Press, 1961.

————(1924), The Economic Problem of Masochism. *Standard Edition,* 19:157-170. London: Hogarth Press, 1961.

————(1925 [1924]), The Resistances to Psycho-Analysis. *Standard Edition,* 19:213-222. London: Hogarth Press, 1961.

————(1926 [1925]), Inhibitions, Symptoms and Anxiety. *Standard Edition,* 20:77-175. London: Hogarth Press, 1959.

————(1930 [1929]), Civilization and Its Discontent. *Standard Edition,* 21:59-145. London: Hogarth Press, 1961.

————(1933 [1932]), New Introductory Lectures on Psycho-Analysis. *Standard Edition,* 22:3-182. London: Hogarth Press, 1964.

————(1937), Analysis Terminable and Interminable. *Standard Edition,* 23:209-253. London: Hogarth Press, 1964.

Greenson, R. R. (1958), Variation in Classical Psycho-Analytic Technique: An Introduction. *International Journal of Psycho-Analysis,* 39:200-201.

Hartmann, E. (1967), *The Biology of Dreaming.* Springfield: Charles C Thomas.

Hartmann, H. (1939), *Ego Psychology and the Problem of Adaptation.* New York: International Universities Press, 1958.

————(1964), *Essays on Ego Psychology.* New York: International Universities Press.

Heimann, P. (1950), On Counter-Transference. *International Journal of Psycho-Analysis,* 31:81-84.

James, M. (1960), Premature Ego Development: Some Observation upon Disturbances in the First

REFERENCES

Three Years of Life. *International Journal of Psycho-Analysis,* 41:288-294.

Kales, A., Hoedemaker, F., Jacobson, A., & Lichtenstein, E. (1964), Dream-deprivation: An Experimental Reappraisal. *Nature* (London), 204: 1337-1338.

Kinsey, A. C. et al. (1948), *Sexual Behavior in the Human Male.* Philadelphia: Saunders.

Klein, M. (1921-1945), *Contributions to Psycho-Analysis.* London: Hogarth Press.

Lampl-de Groot, J. (1967), On Obstacles Standing in the Way of Psychoanalytic Cure. *The Psychoanalytic Study of the Child,* 22:20-35. New York: International Universities Press.

Masters, W. H. & Johnson, V. E. (1966), *Human Sexual Response.* Boston: Little, Brown.

Rapaport, D. & Gill, M. M. (1959), The Points of View and Assumptions of Metapsychology. *International Journal of Psycho-Analysis,* 40:153-162.

Report of the Ad Hoc Committee on Scientific Activities, Heinz Kohut (Chairman), to the Executive Council of the American Psychoanalytic Association, December, 1967.

Rosenfeld, H. (1965), *Psychotic States.* New York: International Universities Press: London: Hogarth Press.

Spitz, R. A. (1956), Transference: The Analytical Setting and Its Prototype. *International Journal of Psycho-Analysis,* 37:380-385.

———(1959), *A Genetic Field Theory of Ego Formation.* New York: International Universities Press.

REFERENCES

————(1965), *The First Year of Life*. New York: International Universities Press.

Strachey, J. (1934), The Nature of the Therapeutic Action of Psycho-Analysis. *International Journal of Psycho-Analysis,* 15:127-159.

————(1937), [Contribution to] Symposium on The Theory of the Therapeutic Results of Psycho-Analysis. *International Journal of Psycho-Analysis,* 18:139-145.

————(1964), Editor's Note [to Analysis Terminable and Interminable (Freud, 1937)]. *Standard Edition,* 23:211-215.

Winnicott, D. W. (1958), *Collected Papers*. New York: Basic Books.

————(1965), *Maturational Processes and the Facilitating Environment*. New York: International Universities Press.

Publications by Dr. Freud

1922

Schlagephantasie und Tagtraum. *Imago,* 8:317-332
  English: The Relation of Beating-Phantasies to a
  Day-Dream. *Int. J. Psa.,* 4:89-102, 1923
  Spanish: Relacion entre fantasias de flagelacion y
  sueño diurno. *Rev. Psicoanál.,* 4:258-271, 1946

1923

Ein hysterisches Symptom bei einem zweieinviertel-
  jährigen Kinde. *Imago,* 9:264-265
  English: An Hysterical Symptom in a Child Two
  years and Three Months Old. *Int. J. Psa.,* 7:227-
  229, 1926

1927

Einführung in die Technik der Kinderanalyse. Leip-
  zig, Vienna, Zurich: Internationaler psychoanalytischer Verlag; London: Imago Publishing Co.,
  1948; Munich: Ernst Reinhardt Verlag, 1966
  English: *Introduction to the Technique of Child
  Analysis.* New York & Washington: Nervous and
  Mental Disease Publishing Co., 1928; also as

Parts I and II in *The Psycho-Analytical Treatment of Children* (1946)

French: Introduction à la psychanalyse des enfants. *Rev. Franç. Psa.*, 4:428-439, 610-633, 1930-1931; 5:71-96, 1932; also as Parts I and II in *Le Traitement psychanalytique des Enfants* (*see sub* 1946)

Dutch, Italian, Spanish, Japanese, Danish: *see sub* 1946

1928

Die Einleitung der Kinderanalyse. *Almanach Psa.*, 187-198; also Ch. 1 in *Einführung in die Technik der Kinderanalyse* (1927)

Zur Theorie der Kinderanalyse. *Int. Z. Psa.*, 14:153-162; also Ch. 6 in *Einführung in die Technik der Kinderanalyse* (1927)

English: On the Theory of Analysis of Children. *Int. J. Psa.*, 10:29-38

1929

Die Beziehungen zwischen Psychoanalyse und Pädagogik. *Z. psa. Päd.*, 3:445-454; also Ch. 4 in *Einführung in die Psychoanalyse für Pädagogen, vier Vorträge* (1930)

Ein Gegenstück zur Tierphobie der Kinder. Abstr.: *Int. Z. Psa.*, 15:518

1930

Einführung in die Psychoanalyse für Pädagogen, vier Vorträge. Stuttgart: Hippokrates; Bern: Huber, 1935; rev., 1956

English: *Introduction to Psycho-Analysis for Teach-*

ers: Four Lectures. London: Allen & Unwin,
1931; and under the title *Psychoanalysis for
Teachers and Parents.* New York: Emerson Books,
1935; Boston: Beacon Press, 1960
Dutch: *Inleiding in de Psycho-Analyse voor Paeda-
gogen.* The Hague: N. V. Boekhandel en Uit-
gevers-Mijh. v. h. W. P. Van Stockum & Zoon,
1932
Italian: *Psicoanalisi per gli Educatori.* Rome: Paolo
Cremonese Editore, 1935

1931

Psychoanalysis of the Child. In: *A Handbook of Child
Psychology,* ed. C. Murchison. Worcester, Mass.:
Clark University Press; London: Oxford Univer-
sity Press, pp. 555-567
German: Psychoanalyse des Kindes. *Z. psa. Päd.,*
6:5-20, 1932; also in *Almanach Psa.,* 177-197, 1933
French: La psychanalyse des enfants. *Rev. Franç.
Psa.,* 13:70-96, 1949

1932

Child Analysis. *The Survey,* 68:398-399, 414-415
German: Erzieher und Neurose. *Z. psa. Päd.,* 6:393-
402

1934

Die Erziehung des Kleinkindes vom psychoanaly-
tischen Standpunkt aus. *Z. psa. Päd.,* 8:17-25; also
in *Almanach Psa.,* 73-84, 1935
English: Psychoanalysis and the Training of the
Young Child. *Psa. Quart.,* 4:15-24, 1935

1935

Ich und Es in der Pubertät. *Z. psa. Päd.,* 9:319-328;
also Ch. XI in *Das Ich und die Abwehrmechanismen* (1936)

1936

Das Ich und die Abwehrmechanismen. Vienna: Inter-
nationaler psychoanalytischer Verlag; London:
Imago Publishing Co., 1946; Munich: Kindler &
Schiermeyer Verlag, 1964

English: *The Ego and the Mechanisms of Defence.*
The International Psycho-Analytical Library, No.
30. London: Hogarth Press & The Institute of
Psycho-Analysis; New York: International Universities Press, 1946; rev. ed., *Writings,** Vol. II
(1966)

French: *Le Moi et les Méchanismes de Défense.*
Paris: Presses Universitaires de France, 1949

Spanish: *El Yo y los Mecanismos de Defensa.* Buenos
Aires: Editorial Medico-Quirurgica, 1949

Italian: *L'Io e i Meccanismi de Difesa.* Florence: G.
Martinelli Editore, 1967

Swedish: *Jaget och dess försvarsmekanismer.* Stockholm: Natur och Kultur, 1969

Finnish: *see sub* 1966

1937

Die Ich-Einschränkung. *Almanach Psa.,* 82-93; also
Ch. VIII in *Das Ich und die Abwehrmechanismen*
(1936)

* The abbreviation *Writings* refers to *The Writings of Anna
Freud,* 7 Volumes (*see sub* date of individual volume)

Triebangst in der Pubertät. *Almanach Psa.,* 94-114; also Ch. XII in *Das Ich und die Abwehrmechanismen* (1936)

1942

(with D. Burlingham) *Young Children in War-Time: A Year's Work in a Residential Nursery.* London: Allen & Unwin; and under the title *War and Children.* New York: Medical War Books, 1943; New York: International Universities Press, 1944

German: *Kriegskinder: Jahresbericht der Kriegskinderheims Hampstead Nurseries.* London: Imago Publishing Co., 1949

Spanish: *La Guerra y los Niños.* Buenos Aires: Editorial Hormé, 1945

1943

(with D. Burlingham) *Infants Without Families: The Case For and Against Residential Nurseries.* London: Allen & Unwin, 1943; new ed., 1965; New York: Medical War Books, 1943; New York: International Universities Press, 1944

Spanish: *Niños sin Hogar.* Buenos Aires: Ediciones Iman, 1947

Swedish: *Barn utan familj.* Stockholm: Kooperativa förbundets bokförlag, 1948

Czech: *Deti bez rodin.* Prague: Obris, 1948

Dutch: *Kindern zonder eigen thuis.* Amsterdam: Scheltema & Holkema's Boekhandel, 1949

French: *Enfants sans Famille.* Paris: Presses Universitaires de France

German: *Anstaltskinder: Argumente fü und gegen*

die Anstaltserziehung von Kleinkindern. London: Imago Publishing Co., 1950
Danish: Arhus: Forlaget Sirius, 1965

1944

Sex in Childhood. *Health Educ. J.,* Vol. 2, No. 1
Difficulties of Sex Enlightenment, *Health Educ. J.,* Vol. 2, No. 2

1945

Indications for Child Analysis. *The Psychoanalytic Study of the Child,* 1:127-149;* also Part III in *The Psycho-Analytical Treatment of Children* (1946); also Ch. 1 in *Writings,* Vol. IV (1968)
French: Indications pour le traitement psychanalytique des enfants. *Rev. Franç. Psa.,* 13:70-96, 1949
German: Indikationsstellung in der Kinderanalyse. *Psyche,* 21:233-253, 1967

1946

Freedom from Want in Early Education. *World Rev.,* 20:(Feb.)36-41; also Ch. 20 in *Writings,* Vol. IV (1968)
The Psychoanalytic Study of Infantile Feeding Disturbances. *The Psychoanalytic Study of the Child,* 2:119-132; also Ch. 2 in *Writings,* Vol. IV (1968)
Problèmes d'adaptation posés par l'education des enfants qui ont souffert de la guerre. *Psyché* (Paris), 1:181-188

* New York: International Universities Press, currently 24 Vols., 1945-1969

The Psycho-Analytical Treatment of Children. London: Imago Publishing Co.; New York: International Universities Press, 1959; New York; Schocken Books, 1964

Dutch: *De psychoanalytische Behandeling van Kindern.* Amsterdam: De Spieghel, 1950

French: *Le Traitement psychanalytique des Enfants.* Paris: Presses Universitaires de France, 1969

Italian: *Psicoanalisi e Bambini.* Milan. Mondadori Editore, 1954

Japanese: Tokyo: Seishin Shobo Co., 1962

Spanish: *Psicoanálisis del Niño.* Buenos Aires: Editorial Hormé, 1964

Danish: Copenhagen: E. Munksgaard, 1965

1947

The Establishment of Feeding Habits. In: *Child Health and Development,* ed. R. W. B. Ellis. London: Churchill, pp. 118-127; also Ch. 21 in *Writings,* Vol. IV (1968)

Emotional and Instinctive Development. In: *Child Health and Development,* ed. R. W. B. Ellis. London: Churchill, pp. 196-215; also, under the title "Emotional and Instinctual Development," as Ch. 22 in *Writings,* Vol. IV (1968)

1948

Sublimation as a Factor in Upbringing. *Health Educ. J.,* Vol. 6, No. 3

Foreword to: H. Sachs, *Masks of Love and Life.* Cambridge, Mass.: Sci-Art

Preface to: H. A. van der Sterren, [*The Adventures of King Oedipus According to the Tragedies of Sophocles*]. Amsterdam: Scheltema & Holkema

1949

Über bestimmte Schwierigkeiten der Elternbeziehung in der Vorpubertät. In: *Die Psychotherapie,* ed. M. Pfister-Amende. Bern: Huber, pp. 10-16

English: On Certain Difficulties in the Preadolescent's Relation to His Parents. Ch. 5 in *Writings,* Vol. IV (1968)

Certain Types and Stages of Social Maladjustment. In: *Searchlights on Delinquency,* ed. K. R. Eissler. New York: International Universities Press: London: Hogarth Press, 1950, pp. 193-204; also in *The Yearbook of Psychoanalysis,** 5:225-237, 1950; also Ch. 4 in *Writings,* Vol. IV (1968)

German: Über bestimmte Phasen und Typen der Dissozialität und Verwahrlosung. In: *Aus der Werkstatt des Erziehungsberaters,* ed. L. Bolterauer. Vienna: Verlag für Jugend und Volk, 1960, pp. 195-206

Aggression in Relation to Emotional Development: Normal and Pathological [1947]. *The Psychoanalytic Study of the Child,* 3/4:37-42; also Ch. 23 in *Writings,* Vol. IV (1968)

Spanish: La agresión en relación con el desarrollo emocional, normal y patológica. *Rev. Psicoanál.,* 7:450-456, 1950

Notes on Aggression. In: *Proceedings of the International Conference on Child Psychiatry* [Interna-

---

* New York: International Universities Press

tional Congress on Mental Health, London, 1948, Vol. II], ed. J. C. Flugel. London: H. K. Lewis; New York: Columbia University Press, pp. 16-23; also in *Bull. Menninger Clin.*, 13:143-151; also in *The Yearbook of Psychoanalysis*, 6:143-154, 1951; in part also in J. Goldstein & J. Katz, *The Family and the Law*. New York: Free Press, 1965, pp. 983-984; also Ch. 3 in *Writings*, Vol. IV (1968)

Some Clinical Remarks Concerning the Treatment of Cases of Male Homosexuality: Summary. *Int. J. Psa.*, 30:195

Nursery School Education: Its Uses and Dangers. *Child Study*, Spring: 35-36, 58-60; also in *Our Children Today*, ed. S. M. Gruenberg et al. New York: Viking Press, 1952, pp. 81-92; also Ch. 26 in *Writings*, Vol. IV (1968)

Foreword to: E. Buxbaum, *Your Child Makes Sense.* New York: International Universities Press: published as a paperback under the title *Understanding Your Child*. New York: Grove Press, 1962; also Ch. 31 in *Writings*, Vol. IV (1968)

1950

Probleme der Lehranalyse [1938]. In: *Max Eitingon in Memoriam*. Jerusalem: Israeli Psychoanalytic Society, pp. 84-94

English: The Problem of Training Analysis. Ch. 19 in *Writings*, Vol. IV (1968)

The Infantile Instinct-Life. In: *Elements of Psychoanalysis*, ed. G. M. Kurth & H. Herma. Cleveland: World Publishing Co., pp. 95-104; and in a paperback under the title *A Handbook of Psychoanaly-*

sis. Cleveland: World Publishing Co., 1963, pp. 95-104

The Significance of the Evolution of Psycho-Analytic Child Psychology. *Congrès International de Psychiatrie, Paris, 1950 Rapports.* Paris: Hermann & Cie., 5:29-36; also Ch. 32 in *Writings,* Vol. IV (1968)

> Spanish: La importancia de la évolucion de la psicologia psicoanálitica de la infancia. *Congrès International de Psychiatrie, Paris, 1950 Rapports.* Paris: Hermann & Cie., 5:37-42

> French: L'importance de l'évolution de la psychologie psychanalytique de l'enfance. *Congrès International de Psychiatrie, Paris, 1950 Rapports.* Paris: Hermann & Cie., 5:43-48

> Italian: Importanza dell'evoluzione della psicologia psicanalitica nell'infanzia. *Cervello,* 27(2):124-126, 1951

1951

Observations on Child Development. *The Psychoanalytic Study of the Child,* 6:18-30; in part also in J. Goldstein & J. Katz, *The Family and the Law.* New York: Free Press, 1965, p. 1060; also Ch. 7 in *Writings,* Vol. IV (1968)

The Contribution of Psychoanalysis to Genetic Psychology. *Amer. J. Orthopsychiat.,* 21:476-497; also Ch. 6 in *Writings,* Vol. IV (1968)

> French: La contribution de la psychanalyse à la psychologie génétique. *Rev. Franç. Psa.,* 20:356-383, 1956

> German: Die Beiträge der Psychoanalyse zur Entwicklungspsychologie. *Psyche,* 11:174-198, 1957

[68]

Obituary: August Aichhorn. *Int. J. Psa.,* 32:51-56; also Ch. 33 in *Writings,* Vol. IV (1968)

(with S. Dann) An Experiment in Group Upbringing. *The Psychoanalytic Study of the Child,* 6:127-168; also in *Readings in Child Development,* ed. W. E. Martin & C. B. Stendler. New York: Harcourt, Brace, 1954, pp. 404-421; also Ch. 8 in *Writings,* Vol. IV (1968)

German: Gemeinschaftsleben im frühen Kindesalter. *Jb. Psa.,* 2:201-248. Köln: Westdeutscher Verlag, 1961/62

1952

Notes on a Connection between the States of Negativism and of Emotional Surrender (*Hörigkeit*). [Author's abstr.]: *Int. J. Psa.,* 33:265; also in Ch. 10, Part II in *Writings,* Vol. IV (1968)

The Mutual Influences in the Development of Ego and Id: Introduction to the Discussion. *The Psychoanalytic Study of the Child,* 7:42-50; also Ch. 9 in *Writings,* Vol. IV (1968)

The Role of Bodily Illness in the Mental Life of Children. *The Psychoanalytic Study of the Child,* 7:69-81; also Ch. 11 in *Writings,* Vol. IV (1968)

French: Le rôle de la maladie somatique dans la vie psychologique des enfants. *Rev. Franç. Psa.,* 21: 631-646, 1957

German: Die Rolle der körperlichen Krankheit im Seelenleben des Kindes. In: *Erziehung in früher Kindheit,* ed. G. Bittner & E. Schmid-Cords. Munich: Piper, 1968, pp. 235-247

The Role of the Teacher. *Harvard Educ. Rev.,* 22: 229-234; also, revised, under the title "Answering

Teachers' Questions," as Ch. 27 in *Writings,* Vol. IV (1968)

Visiting Children: The Child. *Nursing Times,* Vol. 48, No. 13, p. 320, March 29; also Ch. 34 in *Writings,* Vol. IV (1968)

Vorwort der Herausgeber to: Sigmund Freud, *Gesammelte Werke,* Vol. I. London: Imago Publishing Co.

1953

Some Remarks on Infant Observation. *The Psychoanalytic Study of the Child,* 8:9-19; in part also in J. Goldstein & J. Katz, *The Family and the Law.* New York: Free Press, 1965, pp. 871-875; also Ch. 28 in *Writings,* Vol. IV (1968)

The Bearing of the Psychoanalytic Theory of Instinctual Drives on Certain Aspects of Human Behavior [read under the title "Educational and Psychological Techniques for Changing Mental Attitudes Affecting International Understanding" at UNESCO meeting, Paris, 1948]. In: *Drives, Affects, Behavior,* Vol. 1, ed. R. M. Loewenstein. New York: International Universities Press, pp. 259-277; also, under the title "Instinctual Drives and Their Bearing on Human Behavior," as Ch. 24 in *Writings,* Vol. IV (1968)

Film Review of: James Robertson, *A Two-Year-Old Goes to Hospital. Int. J. Psa.,* 34:284-287; also Ch. 12 in *Writings,* Vol. IV (1968)

Introduction to: A. Balint, *The Psycho-Analysis of the Nursery.* London: Routledge & Kegan Paul; and under the title *The Early Years of Life.* New

York: Basic Books, 1954; also Ch. 35 in *Writings,* Vol. IV (1968)

1954

About Losing and Being Lost. [Author's abstr.]: *Int. J. Psa.,* 35:283 [*see also sub* 1967]

The Widening Scope of Indications for Psychoanalysis: Discussion. *J. Amer. Psa. Assn.,* 2:607-620; also Ch. 17 in *Writings,* Vol. IV (1968)

Problems of Infantile Neurosis: A Discussion. *The Psychoanalytic Study of the Child,* 9:25-31, 40-43, 57-62, 68-71; also Ch. 16 in *Writings,* Vol. IV (1968)

Problems of Technique in Adult Analysis. *Bull. Phila. Assn. Psa.,* 4:44-69, also Ch. 18 in *Writings,* Vol. IV (1968)

Psychoanalysis and Education. *The Psychoanalytic Study of the Child,* 9:9-15; also Ch. 15 in *Writings,* Vol. IV (1968)

1955

Safeguarding the Emotional Health of Our Children: An Inquiry into the Concept of the Rejecting Mother. In: *National Conference of Social Work, Casework Papers, 1954.* New York: Family Service Society of America, pp. 5-17; also in *Child Welfare,* 34(3):1-4; also in part in J. Goldstein & J. Katz, *The Family and the Law.* New York: Free Press, 1965, pp. 1059, 1133; also, under the title "The Concept of the Rejecting Mother," as Ch. 29 in *Writings,* Vol. IV (1968); also in *Parenthood: Its Psychology and Psychopathology,* ed. E.

[71]

J. Anthony & T. Benedek. Boston: Little, Brown, 1969 (in press)

1956

The Problem of Aggression and Its Relation to Normal and Pathological Development. *Harofé haivri* [The Hebrew Medical Journal], 50:214-215

Special Experiences of Young Children Particularly in Times of Social Disturbance. In: *Mental Health and Infant Development,* ed. K. Soddy. New York: Basic Books; London: Routledge & Kegan Paul, Vol. I, pp. 141-160

Comments on: Joyce Robertson, A Mother's Observations on the Tonsillectomy of Her Four-Year-Old Daughter. *The Psychoanalytic Study of the Child,* 11:428-432; also Ch. 13 in *Writings,* Vol. IV (1968)

1957

Introduction to: R. A. Spitz, *Die Entstehung der ersten Objektbeziehungen.* Stuttgart: Klett

English: Preface to: R. A. Spitz, *The First Year of Life.* New York: International Universities Press, 1965

Message. In: *1856-1956: Centenaire de la Naissance de Sigmund Freud.* Paris: Presses Universitaires de France, pp. 12-13

Introduction to: A.-M. Sandler, E. Daunton, & A. Schnurmann, Inconsistency in the Mother as a Factor in Character Development. *The Psychoanalytic Study of the Child,* 12:209-210; also Ch. 29 in *Writings,* Vol. V (1969)

Introduction to: G. Casuso, Anxiety Related to the

"Discovery" of the Penis. *The Psychoanalytic Study of the Child,* 12:169-170; also Ch. 28 in *Writings,* Vol. V (1969)

Foreword to: M. Milner, *On Not Being Able to Paint.* London: Heinemann; New York: International Universities Press: also Ch. 33 in *Writings,* Vol. V (1969)

Die Kinderneurose. In: *Das psychoanalytische Volksbuch,* ed. P. Federn & H. Meng. Bern: Huber, pp. 203-214

1958

Clinical Studies in Psycho-Analysis: Research Project of the Hampstead Child-Therapy Clinic. *Proc. Roy. Soc. Med.,* 51:938-942; also in *The Psychoanalytic Study of the Child,* 14:122-131; revised and expanded, under the title "Research Projects of the Hampstead Child-Therapy Clinic," as Ch. 2 in *Writings,* Vol. V (1969)

Child Observation and Prediction of Development: A Memorial Lecture in Honor of Ernst Kris. *The Psychoanalytic Study of the Child,* 13:92-116; in part also in J. Goldstein & J. Katz, *The Family and the Law.* New York: Free Press, 1965, pp. 953-959, 1002, 1017; in part also in J. Katz, J. Goldstein, & A. M. Dershowitz, *Psychoanalysis, Psychiatry and Law.* New York: Free Press, 1967, pp. 399-402; also Ch. 8 in *Writings,* Vol. V (1969)

Adolescence. *The Psychoanalytic Study of the Child,* 13:255-278: also in *Recent Developments in Psychoanalytic Child Therapy,* ed. J. Weinreb. New York: International Universities Press, 1960, pp.

1-24; in part also in J. Goldstein & J. Katz, *The Family and the Law.* New York: Free Press, 1965, pp. 907-908; also Ch. 9 in *Writings,* Vol. V (1969)

German: Probleme der Pubertät. *Psyche,* 14:1-24, 1960

Preface to: T. Freeman, J. L. Cameron, & A. McGhie, *Chronic Schizophrenia.* New York: International Universities Press; London: Tavistock Publications; also Ch. 34 in *Writings,* Vol. V (1969)

1959

Defence Mechanisms. *Encyclopaedia Britannica.* Chicago, London, Toronto: William Benton; also in subsequent editions

1960

The Child Guidance Clinic as a Center of Prophylaxis and Enlightenment [1957]. In: *Recent Developments in Psychoanalytic Child Therapy,* ed. J. Weinreb. New York: International Universities Press, pp. 25-38; also Ch. 17 in *Writings,* Vol. V (1969)

Why Children Go Wrong. In: *The Enrichment of Childhood.* London: The Nursery School Association of Great Britain and Northern Ireland, pp. 23-34; also, under the title "Entrance into Nursery School: The Psychological Prerequisites," as Ch. 19 in *Writings,* Vol. V (1969)

Discussion of Dr. John Bowlby's Paper [Grief and Mourning in Infancy and Early Childhood]. *The Psychoanalytic Study of the Child,* 15:53-62; also Ch. 10, Part II in *Writings,* Vol. V (1969)

Introduction to: K. Levy. Simultaneous Analysis of a Mother and Her Adolescent Daughter. *The Psychoanalytic Study of the Child,* 15:378-380; also Ch. 30 in *Writings,* Vol. V (1969)

Foreword to: M. Ruben, *Parent Guidance in the Nursery School.* New York: International Universities Press; also Ch. 35 in *Writings,* Vol. V (1969)

Geleitwort zum *Johrbuch der Psychoanalyse.* Köln: Westdeutscher Verlag

1961

Paediatricians' Questions and Answers. In: *Psychosomatic Aspects of Paediatrics,* ed. R. MacKeith & J. Sandler. London: Pergamon Press, pp. 27-41; also, under the title "Answering Pediatricians' Questions," as Ch. 23 in *Writings,* Vol. V (1969)

1962

Assessments of Normality and Pathology. In: *Clinical Problems of Young Children: The Proceedings of the 18th Child Guidance Inter-Clinic Conference.* London: National Association for Mental Health, pp. 22-29; also, under the title "Clinical Problems of Young Children," as Ch. 21 in *Writings,* Vol. V (1969)

The Emotional and Social Development of Young Children. Report of the 9th World Assembly, London, July 16-21, 1962 (World Organisation for Early Childhood Education, Organisation Mondiale pour l'éducation préscholaire); also Ch. 20 in *Writings,* Vol. V (1969)

The Theory of the Parent-Infant Relationship: Contribution to Discussion. *Int. J. Psa.,* 43:240-242; also Ch. 11 in *Writings,* Vol. V (1969)

Assessment of Childhood Disturbances. *The Psychoanalytic Study of the Child,* 17:149-158; in part also in *Normality and Pathology in Childhood* (1965), pp. 140-147

1963

Regression as a Principle in Mental Development. *Bull. Menninger Clin.,* 27:126-139; also, revised, in *Normality and Pathology in Childhood* (1965), pp. 93-107; in part also in J. Goldstein & J. Katz, *The Family and the Law.* New York: Free Press, 1965, pp. 903-904; in part also in J. Katz, J. Goldstein, & A. M. Dershowitz, *Psychoanalysis, Psychiatry and Law.* New York: Free Press, 1967, pp. 351-353

The Concept of Developmental Lines. *The Psychoanalytic Study of the Child,* 18:245-265; also, revised, in *Normality and Pathology in Childhood* (1965), pp. 62-87

The Role of Regression in Mental Development. In: *Modern Perspectives in Child Development,* ed. A. J. Solnit & S. A. Provence, New York: International Universities Press, pp. 97-106; also Ch. 24 in *Writings,* Vol. V (1969)

1964

Foreword to: A. Aichhorn, *Delinquency and Child Guidance: Selected Papers,* ed. O. Fleischmann, P. Kramer, & H. Ross. New York: International Universities Press

1965

Normality and Pathology in Childhood: Assessments of Development. New York: International Universities Press; London: Hogarth Press, 1966; also *Writings,* Vol. VI (1969)

German: *Wege und Irrwege in der Kinderentwicklung*. Bern & Stuttgart: Huber & Klett, 1968

French: *Le Normal et le Pathologique chez l'Enfant*. Paris: Éditions Gallimard, 1968

Danish: *Normalitet og patologi i barndommen*. Copenhagen: Han Reitzels, 1968

Swedish: *Barnets psykiska hälsa*. Stockholm: Bokförlaget Prisma, 1967

Italian: Milan: Giangiacomo Feltrinelli Editore (in press)

Spanish: Buenos Aires: Ediciones Siglo Veinte (in press)

(with T. Bergmann) *Children in the Hospital*. New York: International Universities Press; Foreword and "Conclusion" also Ch. 25 in *Writings,* Vol. V (1969)

Diagnostic Skills and Their Growth in Psycho-Analysis. *Int. J. Psa.,* 46:31-38; in part also in *Normality and Pathology in Childhood* (1965), pp. 11-24

Some Recent Developments in Child Analysis. *Psychotherapy and Psychosomatics,* 13:36-46. Basel & New York: Karger

Heinz Hartmann: A Tribute. *J. Amer. Psa. Assn.,* 13:195-196; also Ch. 36 in *Writings,* Vol. V (1969)

On the Difficulties of Communicating with Children. In J. Goldstein & J. Katz, *The Family and the Law*. New York: Free Press, pp. 261-264, 960-962,

1051-1053; in part also in J. Katz, J. Goldstein, & A. M. Dershowitz, *Psychoanalysis, Psychiatry and Law*. New York. Free Press, 1967, pp. 417-419; also, under the title "Three Contributions to a Seminar on Family Law," as Ch. 26 in *Writings*, Vol. V (1969)

The Hampstead Child-Therapy Clinic: An Informal Seminar. Washington: National Institute of Child Health and Human Development, National Institutes of Health

Foreword to: J. Lampl-de Groot, *The Development of the Mind*. New York: International Universities Press; London: Hogarth Press; also Ch. 37 in *Writings*, Vol. V (1969)

Preface to: J. Bolland, J. Sandler et al., *The Hampstead Psychoanalytic Index*. New York: International Universities Press; London: Hogarth Press; also Ch. 31 in *Writings*, Vol. V (1969)

French: Paris: Presses Universitaires de France (in press)

(with H. Nagera & W. E. Freud) Metapsychological Assessment of the Adult Personality: The Adult Profile. *The Psychoanalytic Study of the Child*, 20:9-41; in part also Ch. 4 in *Writings*, Vol. V (1969)

1966

The Writings of Anna Freud, Volume II (1936). *The Ego and the Mechanisms of Defense*, rev. ed. New York: International Universities Press; London: Hogarth Press, 1967

Finnish: *Minän suo-jautumiskeinot*. Helsinki: Weilin & Göös, 1969

Some Thoughts about the Place of Psychoanalytic Theory in the Training of Psychiatrists. *Bull. Menninger Clin.,* 30:225-234; to be included in *Writings,* Vol. VII

A Short History of Child Analysis. *The Psychoanalytic Study of the Child,* 21:7-14; to be included in *Writings,* Vol. VII

Links between Hartmann's Ego Psychology and the Child Analyst's Thinking [1964]. In: *Psychoanalysis—A General Psychology,* ed. R. M. Loewenstein, L. M. Newman, M. Schur, & A. J. Solnit. New York: International Universities Press, pp. 16-27; also Ch. 13 in *Writings,* Vol. V (1969)

Obsessional Neurosis: A Summary of Psycho-Analytic Views as Presented at the Congress. *Int. J. Psa.,* 47:116-122; also Ch. 15 in *Writings,* Vol. V (1969)

Interactions between Nursery School and Child Guidance Clinic. *J. Child Psychother.,* 1:40-44; also Ch. 22 in *Writings,* Vol. V (1969)

Foreword to: *Sex and the College Student,* formulated by the Committee on the College Student, Group for the Advancement of Psychiatry, ed. H. P. Eddy. New York: Atheneum; to be included in *Writings,* Vol. VII

Foreword to: H. Nagera, *Early Childhood Disturbances, the Infantile Neurosis, and the Adulthood Disturbances.* New York: International Universities Press; London: Hogarth Press; also Ch. 32 in *Writings,* Vol. V (1969)

Italian: *La Nevrosi Infantile.* Rome: Armando Armando Editore (in press)

Spanish: Buenos Aires: Editorial Hormé (in press)

[79]

1967

About Losing and Being Lost [1953]. *The Psychoanalytic Study of the Child,* 22:9-19; also Ch. 14 in *Writings,* Vol. IV (1968)

    German: Über Verlieren und Verlorengehen. In: *Hoofdstukken uit de Hedendaagse Psychoanalyse,* ed. P. J. van der Leeuw, E. C. M. Frijling-Schreuder, & P. C. Kuiper. Arnem: Van Loghum & Slaterus, pp. 91-100

Comments on Trauma [1964]. In: *Psychic Trauma,* ed. S. S. Furst. New York: Basic Books, pp. 235-245; also, revised and expanded, under the title "Comments on Psychic Trauma," as Ch. 14 in *Writings,* Vol. V (1969)

Eine Diskussion mit René Spitz. *Psyche,* 21:4-15

    English: A Discussion with René Spitz. To be included in *Writings,* Vol. VII

Doctoral Award Address [1964]. *J. Amer. Psa. Assn.,* 15:833-840; also Ch. 38 in *Writings,* Vol. V (1969)

Preface to: H. Nagera, *Vincent van Gogh.* London: Allen & Unwin. New York: International Universities Press; to be included in *Writings,* Vol. VII

Comments on the First Day's Reports. In: *On Rearing Infants and Young Children in Institutions.* Washington: Children's Bureau Research Reports, No. 1, pp. 47-55

1968

The Writings of Anna Freud, Volume IV (1945-1956): *Indications for Child Analysis and Other Papers.* New York: International Universities Press; London: Hogarth Press, 1969

Obituary: Willie Hoffer. *The Psychoanalytic Study of the Child,* 23:7-9; to be included in *Writings,* Vol. VII

Expert Knowledge for the Average Mother [1949]. Ch. 25 in *Writings,* Vol. IV (1968)

Studies in Passivity [1952]. Ch. 10 in *Writings,* Vol. IV (1968)

Indications and Contraindications for Child Analysis. *The Psychoanalytic Study of the Child,* 23:37-46; to be included in *Writings,* Vol. VII

The Sleeping Difficulties of the Young Child: An Outline [1947]. Ch. 30 in *Writings,* Vol. IV (1968)

Acting Out. *Int. J. Psa.,* 49:165-170; to be included in *Writings,* Vol. VII

Vorwort to: S. Freud, *Gesammelte Werke,* Vol. 18: *Gesamtregister.* Frankfurt am Main: S. Fischer

1969

The Writings of Anna Freud, Volume V (1956-1965): *Research at the Hampstead Child-Therapy Clinic and Other Papers.* New York: International Universities Press; London: Hogarth Press, 1970

Obituary: James Strachey. *Int. J. Psa.* (in press)

The Writings of Anna Freud, Volume VI (1965): *Normality and Pathology in Childhood: Assessments of Development.* New York: International Universities Press

The Hampstead Child-Therapy Course and Clinic [1957]. Ch. I in *Writings,* Vol. V (1969)

Assessment of Pathology in Childhood [1962, 1964, 1965]. Ch. 3 in *Writings,* Vol. V (1969)

Psychoanalysis and Family Law [1964]. Ch. 5 in *Writings,* Vol. V (1969)

Services for Underprivileged Children [1966]. Ch. 6 in *Writings,* Vol. V (1969)

The Contribution of Direct Child Observation to Psychoanalysis [1957]. Ch. 7 in *Writings,* Vol. V (1969)

Discussion Remarks to Dr. John Bowlby's Paper on "Separation Anxiety" [1958]. Ch. 10, Part I in *Writings,* Vol. V (1969)

An Appreciation of Herman Nunberg [1964]. Ch. 12 in *Writings,* Vol. V (1969)

Psychoanalytic Knowledge Applied to the Rearing of Children [1956]. Ch. 16 in *Writings,* Vol. V (1969)

The Assessment of Borderline Cases [1956]. Ch. 18 in *Writings,* Vol. V (1969)

Psychoanalytic Knowledge and Its Application to Children's Services [1964]. Ch. 27 in *Writings,* Vol. V (1969)

Adolescence as a Developmental Disturbance [1966]. In: *Adolescence: Psychosocial Perspectives,* ed. G. Caplan & S. Lebovici. New York: Basic Books, pp. 5-11; to be included in *Writings,* Vol. VII

Film Review: *John, 17 Months, Nine Days in a Residential Nursery,* by James and Joyce Robertson. *The Psychoanalytic Study of the Child,* 24 (in press)

1970

The Writings of Anna Freud, Volume VII (1966-1970). New York: International Universities Press (in press)

In Preparation

The Writings of Anna Freud, Volume I (1922-1935), will contain *Introduction to the Technique of Child Analysis* (1927), *Psychoanalysis for Teachers and Parents* (1930), both in revised translations, as well as the writer's first psychoanalytic papers.

The Writings of Anna Freud, Volume III (1937-1944), written with Dorothy Burlingham will contain *War and Children* (1943), *Infants Without Families* (1944), and selections from the previously unpublished monthly reports on the work at the Hampstead War Nurseries.